TEN LAWS
OF
UNLIMITED SUCCESS
Workbook

Cecilia B. Loving

Myrtle Tree Press LLC
Brooklyn, NY
www.myrtletreepress.webs.com

ISBN 13 - 978-0-9799247-9-8
ISBN 10 - 0-9799247-9-0

Book sales for North America and international:
Myrtle Tree Press LLC
376 President Street, Suite 2H
Brooklyn, New York 11231
Phone: 718-596-8019 (toll free 1-800-940-9642)
Fax: 888-583-7086; email orders to myrtletreepressllc@gmail.com

Printed in the United States of America

"It didn't matter what mistakes were made;
it didn't matter who wished him ill;
it didn't matter who tried to interfere;
it didn't even matter if he were the victim
of some trumped-up charge. . . .
He was going to succeed.
He was going to triumph.
He was going to let the pure synergy of force carry him. . . .
[H]e would rise to the top,
above everything that came at him."

from *God is a Lawyer Too: Ten Laws of Unlimited Success*

CONTENTS

ACKNOWLEDGMENTS

A special thanks to
Paula Brown-Donaldson,
the Practicing Attorneys for Law Students, Inc.,
and Patterson Belknap Webb & Tyler LLP,
all of whom helped me realize the need to write this book; and to
my husband Marlon Cromwell who supports me in every endeavor;
my parents Myrtle and Hicey Ross who help me discern the voice within;
my SPIRITMUV family Raquiba LaBrie, Elizabeth Walker, Najah Brown,
Lorraine Dowd-Snella, Johar Snella, Nan Baldwin, Judi Ventress, Sheri Bailey,
Andrea Hibbert, Electra Fulbright, Christina Lawrence, Kelly Dobbs,
Esther Sylvester, Bianca Townsend, Maurice, Avanti and Azalia Brown,
Christopher, Carla, Christa, and Camille Loving,
who help me grow as a teacher and a student of truth;
my editor Rick Taylor, whose compassion and fortitude embrace these words;
my friends Vaughn Browne, Haneefah Jackson, Femi Austin,
Denise Quarles, Lia Brooks, Bayliss Fiddiman,
and all of the other law students and lawyers
who inspired this book;
and to the unlimited power of success
– always waiting to bless us
especially if we obey its laws.

1 THE LAW OF BELIEVING IN OURSELVES

> *"All things are possible to him that believeth,"* Dale said. *"If someone asked you if you believe, what would you say?"*
>
> *"I would say yes, I believe,"* Najih said slowly, trying to anticipate where the conversation was going.
>
> *"But the question is,"* Dale asked, *"what do you believe in?"*

Every chapter of our life is different. Each chapter provides a challenge which is more often than not a disguised opportunity. Each opportunity provides the experience to learn a spiritual principle. Each spiritual principle is a law of success. If we discern it, learn it and master it – we succeed. But there is a difference between mere achievement and succeeding through the application of spiritual laws. True success does not merely require that we reach our goals. The accomplishment of our goals only accounts for part of our success. True success lies in the process of spiritual growth rather than the mere manifestation of material things. We are not merely here to make a lot of money or own a lot of material goods but to be the best people we can be. We cannot be as good as we can unless we realize our true worth; unless we know to expect the best; unless we defy the appearances around us to believe in ourselves.

Our calling, be it in the legal field or some other profession, is just one avenue to help us evolve into better people. No matter what the universe calls us to do, our lights shine their brightest when we believe in our ability to succeed. No matter what the obstacles, we succeed when we believe that we can. Do we believe that we can get the job that we want? Do we believe that we can leave our current job? Do we believe that we can return to the workforce? Do we believe that these ten laws of unlimited success will help us succeed? Are we ready to change our consciousness? If so, these exercises will teach us how to:

1. Succeed by believing that we will;
2. Love our way to success by transcending negativity;
3. Center in success daily by tapping the power within us;
4. Release the past and tell a new story of our success;
5. Create the opportunities that we desire;
6. Speak truth to power by claiming our success with every word that we utter;
7. Envision success with our ability to see absolute good;
8. Shine our light of success in every aspect of our being;
9. Accept our victory without hesitation, fear or doubt; and
10. Do even greater things than we could ever imagine.

Everything is always available to us in a vast universe of unlimited good. When we say, "I believe," we enter a consciousness that makes us more receptive to the good that is always in our midst. When we say "I believe," we connect with the inexhaustible source that is everywhere present around us – in the air that we breathe and the space that we take up, the wholeness of which we are an individualized part. We believe when we can actually perceive the unlimited nature of absolute good. If we are believers, then the absolute good around us no longer seems far-fetched. If we stop what we are doing right now, and say "I believe," we automatically change the vibration of our thoughts and open the channels of the good in which we live and move and have our being. We enter a moment in consciousness when we truly connect with unlimited source, which is the *wholeness* of which we all participate as individuals. Some call this source God, but it doesn't matter what we call it. The most important thing is realizing that source wants nothing more than to bless us – to teach that there is no separation between us and the good that is seeking us.

We can succeed right here, right now – but we have to learn to see beyond the appearances – beyond everything that we see with the physical eye. In the physical realm, there is always lack and limitation. But we are not limited to the physical. We are not just human, we are also divine. Our humanness is merely a shell, the temple covering the divine in us. When we believe, we know that we are so much more than our bodies; we are also our souls. Our flesh, or our body temple, is just the tool that we were blessed with to be able to better accomplish our good. Every gift, every talent, every challenge, every opportunity that we have are all part of what allows the universe to express as us.

We are not the sum total of our achievements or lack thereof; we are pure potential awaiting unlimited success. We are not average; we are not mediocre; we are not marginal. We are not too young or too old. We are not our current jobs or the jobs that we desire. We are more than our schools, our grades, or our associations. We are not our neighborhoods, our ethnic groups or our religions. We are everything that we need to manifest the change that we want to see take place in the world.

When we believe, we are so well aware that our good is manifesting that we do not have to wait to give thanks. We can be grateful for what has yet to manifest now. Knowing requires us to believe that even before we formulate a desire, it is already taking place in the physical realm. Knowing is the key that opens infinite channels of good that will give way to our desires. By the time we perceive that we have a need, absolute good has gone before us so that the answer, the resources, the power that we need is already revealing itself to us. When we believe that we will receive, what we need is on its way.

Asking is part of believing. We can ask the universe for whatever we want, but we have to believe that we will get it. Everyone has the power to ask, but even those who do, do not really believe that they will receive. Belief requires us to know that we will get what we ask for. Doubt is the opposite of belief. Doubt is complaining, fretting, worrying, and procrastinating when the only thing that we should be doing is believing, knowing and trusting that our blessings are unfolding.

When we ask the universe for what we want, we cannot have even the slightest, the smallest, the most miniscule bit of doubt. We have to ask with confidence, courage and boldness. When we fail to ask for what we really know in our heart that we desire, we slow down the flow of our good. Our disbelief creates the barriers that keep the channels of our good closed. It's important to keep them open because the things that we desire are not just for us. Millions of people – those we do know and those yet to be born – can benefit from the things that we teach, write, invent, create, build, display, or design. We are called to manifest good for people we have never met and never will meet. We are just one of the universe's many instruments of change. If we hold back from asking for what we want and believing that we will receive it, we create an illusion of lack that not only impacts us but all of those who stand to benefit from what we were called to do.

We live in a universe that has no time, no limitation, no lack. We create these constraints in our consciousness. We say that we don't have time. We believe that we cannot go the distance. We stop short of our true potential. We hinder ourselves because of fear. Every time we believe there is lack, we should look at those who have. We should look at the vast resources around us. The supply to meet our demands is right where we are and exactly what we need. All we have to do is knock; the door to opportunity is always open. When we come inside, it may not appear to look like what we expected at first. There may be a bit of messiness involved. There may be a few more hills to climb. The process of growing through the lessons that life has to teach may surprise us, but what we want is always there – waiting for us to pursue it.

The universe can do no more for us than it can do through us. We can't worry about not meeting someone else's expectations. We can't worry about what the neighbors might say. We can't worry about what other people may think. When we spend our energy telling people about our plans, we have little energy left to pursue them. Other people's vibrations of fear and envy can interfere with our ability to demonstrate our good. We start to take on their doubts, their anxieties and their worries. We get excited and want to share our desires with others, but talking about something before it has manifested diffuses our energy. We have to be careful, really careful of those we share with – that person has to be a believer as well. If they are not in accord with our belief, they will drain our energy, diffuse our enthusiasm and distract our focus.

When we believe, we trust that we will receive what seems impossible on the outside. When we believe, we ask the universe for what we want – using enough detail to see it with clarity. We need clarity, as well as heartfelt and deep desire. We need the ability to release our desires – trusting that whatever we want is already on its way to us. Belief is the most important law of unlimited success. Without it, we can see what we want and claim what we want, but if we don't believe that we will receive it, we won't.

MY PERSONAL MISSION STATEMENT

_____
_____
_____
_____
_____
_____
_____
_____
_____
_____
_____
_____
_____
_____

10 THINGS TO HELP ACCOMPLISH MY PERSONAL MISSION

1._____
2._____
3._____
4._____
5._____
6._____
7._____
8._____
9._____
10._____

ACCOUNTABILITY PARTNER/S

_____
_____
_____
_____

I ASK THE UNIVERSE AND BELIEVE I WILL RECEIVE

_____
_____
_____
_____

AFFIRMATION OF SUCCESS

AFFIRMATION OF BELIEF

I believe that there is a Power within me that lovingly directs me to perfect health, perfect relationships, a perfect career, perfect peace, perfect prosperity of every kind.

I believe that my desires are my good seeking me.

I believe that I am worthy to receive what I ask for.

I believe that I deserve Absolute Good in every shape, form or dimension that I desire.

I believe that I can move forward with my life, by not being a victim of the past, by creating a new life for myself, by embracing the Power within.

I believe that this is the moment that will change my life: the point of power is in the present moment. There is not and never will be another moment like this one.

I will use the appearances of any temporary setback to energize me — so that no matter what happens, I will make an even greater effort.

I will release any negative interlopers, toxic talkers or pity-partiers who could potentially drain my energy, diminish my momentum or re-direct my focus.

I believe that I am divinely guided — and I may not understand everything that is happening around me just based on what I see in the physical realm, but despite what I see in the physical, I know I am in my right place, at my right time, doing the right thing.

I believe that everything I need to know to attain my good is revealed to me.

I believe that the right people show up at the right time to help me.

I believe that the right situations and circumstances unfold at their right time, in their right place.

I won't let a single day pass without making at least one definite movement towards the accomplishment of my goals.

I will expect the best as I only receive what I believe.

2 THE LAW OF LOVING BEYOND FEAR

"Love allows us to be in control – no matter what the situation," Dale said. "Even when someone mistreats us or talks about us or otherwise attempts to marginalize us, love wins the day."

Olga chimed in, "de one who lub de moorse win." For some reason, her words always hit Najih in a profound way: "the one who loves the most wins."

Love is the most powerful energy we have to attract our good to us. Love gives us the ability to attract what we want when we want it. When we use the energy of love in our daily affairs, it requires that we give – that we allow harmony, peace and compassion to flow from us, and it is the process of giving that attracts all that we desire. Love creates all good. Love heals all things. Love manifests all desires. If we could work with only one law of unlimited success, it should be love. With love, we would have everything we desire in no time.

Two people focused on the same goals are always better than one. Two or more gathered in the strength of love will energize their success in a more immediate way. We don't need another person to activate the power of love. We don't need a spouse or a partner to be able to manifest what we want. But if we have a spiritual partner, we have a master mind – a combined force of focus and extra energy to tap into. That's why some people form master mind groups. The focused energy of others in a loving like-minded fashion brings better results. But it has to be based in love: if it is based on fear, competition or envy, it will be more destructive than productive. We are all expressions of love in action. We all form love's infinite channels of good. We are each here to provide everyone with the ability to succeed. Love is the most important aspect of our being. Love will move any mountain. Love will heal any relationship. Love will solve any problem. No matter what we do, if we put love first, we will reap the most amazing results. Love will move our enemies out of the way. Send them love and either they will change before our very eyes, or they will disappear into the ethers from which they came.

Love shouldn't be a struggle. We have to put love before money. The irony is that when we do, love supplies everything that we need. We have to put love before our own particular needs. When we do, love will carry the day and the rest will sort itself out. This type of love is not about romance, or love in the flesh. This is about love in the Spirit. When we are truly loving, we don't fail to do what we can to try to help other people. True love does not interfere with helping people. We must start by loving ourselves because if we don't have the capacity to love ourselves, we won't know how to give love to someone else.

Love is not the happily-ever-after fairy tale that we learn about in grade school. Love is here as part of the daily grind, the constant struggle and the rigorous strife to plant new seeds, create new passages, and divine new purposes. Love appears in endless guises, including the least-expected challenge or the worst fight of our lives. Love lessons teach us how to be better people. Love requires that we do good unto others. Love requires that we be decent and respectful, even when we'd like to be rude and selfish. Love requires that we take the high road. Love requires that we go with the flow – just like water. What does water do? It doesn't try to move any obstacle out of the way; it flows around it. Water will flow right past a mountain, as though it wasn't even there. Love is the same way; it can move through any challenge as though it wasn't there. Everything can be resolved with love. Love is the strongest healing power that there is. If we don't have the strength, or the energy, or the courage to do something, we can just call on love. Love is available to do the heavy-lifting. If we just sit down and think thoughts of love, feel love and send love as an energy coming from us – directed to someone or something else, we create a lasting energy of success. Meditation and prayer with loving thoughts creates success. Any time that we have a tendency to think negatively about anything or anyone, we can send them love instead, and that energy of love will not only bless them, it will bless us.

Love is limitless. It has no boundaries. It has no greed, no expectations, no distrust. Love is not pretentious. Love is honest, pure, open and receptive. Love is not about *finding* the right person, but being the right person. Love is the only fulfillment that we can possibly get in life. Money, material things, even relationships are merely the by-products of love.

Loving relationships with other people teach us how to grow spiritually because relationships require sacrifice, devotion, peace and harmony, but the relationships themselves are not the ultimate goal. What is more important is to understand our oneness – our endless connection with the power of love. Relationships are simply the vehicle to express our love. Relationships are the training grounds for strengthening love.

Love helps establish order. As long as we act out of a consciousness of love, we will be guided correctly. Not only will the right people show up, but we will be in the right consciousness to receive their help.

Sometimes the greatest love that we can show is through the power of surrender. Even those people we dislike have to be loved. We can only love them by surrendering to the power of love. But the one who loves the most wins. Loving the most means blessing our jobs and always commanding excellence regardless of whether it is what we want to do. We have to love and bless our jobs, even the jobs that we hate; we have to love and bless whatever we are doing now. We have to bless every single aspect of the workplace and each individual in it.

When we surrender to love, we will discover that all of the worries, all of the concerns, all of the cares, and all of the reactions that we have to the world around us will disappear. We will be focused on what we can bring to the picture, how we can advance the best contribution possible. Love will shine through us with a radiance that is born from simply being in a universe of unlimited possibility. Love will strengthen us with the understanding that nothing and no one can stop us from getting our greatest good.

Love requires us to put forth more than a concerted effort. Love requires that we go the extra mile and do more than is required. This is applicable to any profession. We have to master what needs to get done in whatever field we are in. Loving our profession empowers us to do more, give more, be more.

Love has many channels. We never know who will show up in our life to teach us the power of love. Love is not about taking. The more love we give, the more love we receive. Love is a magnet of the universe – attracting everything and everyone that we need in perfect divine order. We will soon learn that we actually give and receive simultaneously. There is no waiting. With love, we can see the immediate manifestation of our good taking place.

Love gets rid of all fear, all doubt, all worry, all pain, all anxiety – as well as anything, any place and anyone who does not fully support us in whatever it is that we choose to do.

Love is bigger than any condition in the flesh. Love is the vortex of all creation re-creating out of itself without limitation. Love is the only real success there is.

HEALING WITH THE ENERGY OF LOVE

List 10 Fears About Your Career, Relationships, etc.

1._____

2._____

3._____

4._____

5._____

6._____

7._____

8._____

9._____

10._____

LOVE MEDITATION

Pull fear out of the pit of your stomach,
from your heart
from your soul,
from every aspect of your being.

Surround each item with love,
peace and healing energy
— without reservation.
Surrender fear to the wind,
to space, to nothingness, to air.

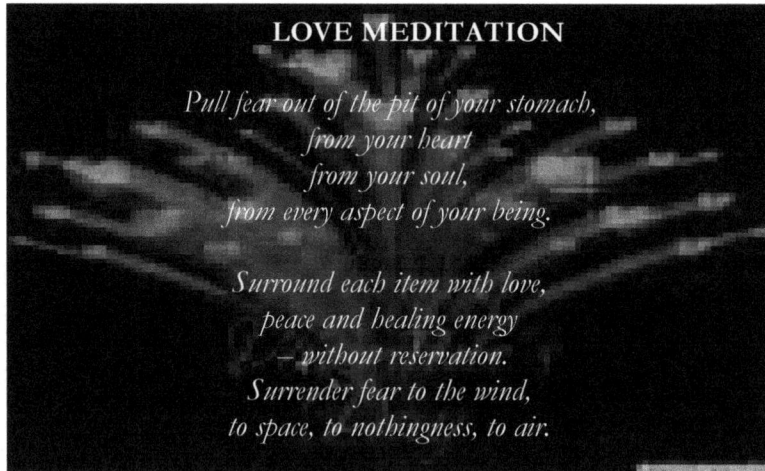

REFLECTIONS ON HEALING WITH THE ENERGY OF LOVE

_____
_____
_____
_____
_____
_____
_____
_____

ACCOUNTABILITY PARTNER/S

_____
_____
_____
_____

LOVING ACTS THAT WE CAN DO FOR THOSE WE KNOW

_____
_____
_____
_____
_____
_____
_____
_____
_____
_____

RANDOM ACTS OF KINDNESS

_____
_____
_____
_____
_____
_____
_____
_____
_____
_____
_____

WAYS TO LOVE OURSELVES

_____
_____
_____
_____
_____
_____
_____
_____
_____

THOUGHTS ON A LOVING ATTITUDE

A loving attitude is a success attitude. Love is an energy that emanates confidence because we are clear that we have something to offer. It is a wisdom that exudes accomplishment rather than doubt. A loving attitude empowers us to attract the best opportunities to us.

A loving attitude is one that is secure about its goals, talents and skills. A loving attitude is one that is centered in the truth that it cannot fail. People with a loving attitude do not get caught up in the woes and pity parties and drama of other people, but direct their energy in a positive vein – without worry, distress, anxiety, or frustration. They know that no one has the power to determine their destiny. Everyone around them can feel the strength of the energy emanating and filling their presence.

A loving attitude is creative. All of us are creative but some of us fail to tap our inner wisdom for the right solution, thereby never exercising our creativity. Our own creativity will often provide us with the most favorable outcome. The most important thing is to trust our own judgment. Our view, our solution, our proposal may not be agreed with or be followed or adopted. But if we do not articulate it or follow up on it, we fail to give what only we can provide.

A loving attitude takes charge of life. Taking charge means giving the situation our very best. It means not waiting on others. It means educating ourselves as much as possible about whatever it is that we want to do. It means pushing ourselves outside our comfort zones to meet people and make connections, to get opportunities, to volunteer, to do whatever we realize will help us achieve our goals. Taking charge of our goals requires energy, commitment, discipline, and focus. We have to create a plan of action; prioritize our time and obligations; discipline ourselves to commit to our plan; and put our energy into whatever it is that needs to be done.

A loving attitude is a grateful one. We must give thanks for the experiences and opportunities that we get, and accord the proper praise and thanks to others. The most successful people take time to send thank-you notes — even just to say thanks for being my friend, or thanks for joining me for dinner. Our classmates or fellow associates today are the leaders who will assume major roles of responsibility tomorrow. Regardless, they should always be thanked.

The question is how to cultivate a loving attitude, improve it, maintain it, or even reverse a reaction to someone else's negative energy into a positive, self-affirming attitude. By understanding that love develops from the inside out: the stronger our inner foundation, the better prepared we will be for any external challenge. A loving attitude is charitable; it gives by understanding that it has nothing to lose. Whatever is given to others ultimately comes back. Giving is kindness and courtesy, compassion and understanding. This means if a fellow colleague has a need, we give. If an employer desires, we go the extra mile. Giving, however, begins with us. We have to make sure that we are at our best and have first taken care of our needs, which makes us better-suited to give to others. With a loving attitude, the job is ours, the victory is ours, the success is ours — because we will radiate success, which is what any employer or client wants — a winner.

3 THE LAW OF CENTERING DAILY

"One of the most important laws of success is to stay centered. You have to make sure that you center daily. Then, you won't be vulnerable to the things that go on around you," Dale said.

"What does centering do?" Najih asked.

"Centering allows you to align to the absolute good of the universe. You can center through meditation, through prayer, through movement, through music, through silence, even through reading inspirational things," Dale continued. "When you center, you surrender to the power that is greater than what you see in the physical. . . . Finding our connection with the universe — regardless of what you choose to call it is not a one-time experience, it is a daily practice."

We center through meditation, through prayer, through movement, through music, through silence, and even through reading inspirational things. When we center, we surrender to the power that is greater than what we see in the physical. We can center through our religion or none at all — just a nondenominational love for all things. Most people get so caught up in the rituals of religion — signing the cross or kneeling at command or even taking communion — that they sometimes forget what these sacraments are for and do them without internalizing them in their minds, bodies and souls. Centering returns us to the heart of what most religious rituals symbolize, which is our divine connection to the love, peace, prosperity, wholeness, and joy of the universe. Finding our connection with the universe — regardless of what we choose to call it is not a one-time experience, it is a daily practice. We can center in release, center in wholeness, center in abundance, center in creativity.

Centering allows us to trust that our good is taking shape. No matter how much work we do in the direction of our dreams, at some point, we have to let go. When we wake up in the morning, we must breathe in our connection to inexhaustible supply – however we perceive it. Some people perceive it as God. Some people perceive it as themselves. It doesn't matter what we call it. What matters is that we realize that there is a power within us that is everywhere present.

Breathing is powerful. One particular breathing exercise that everyone should use is an alternative nostril breathing – or *Anuloma Viloma* in Hindu, alternating the flow of our breath or *prana* through one nostril and out the other one. This practice enhances balance in our life, especially with regard to our male and female energy. We do have both. It also helps us access the universe in a manner that centers us. This is always done in a ratio of 1:4:2 – so if we inhale for a count of four; then we hold for a count of sixteen; and we exhale to a count of eight.

We have to use our right hand, and place our middle and index finger on our right palm. This is called the *Vishnu Mudra* and is known to direct energy. It may be hard to do because our ring finger usually likes to follow our middle finger. We use our thumb to block the right nostril and our baby finger and ring finger to block the left side of our nostril.

There are six stages of breathing. *First*, block the right nostril and inhale through the left. *Second*, hold the breath and remove both hands. *Third*, block the left nostril and exhale through the right. *Fourth*, inhale through the right nostril and block the left nostril. *Fifth*, hold the breath – blocking both of our nostrils. *Sixth*, block the right nostril, and exhale through the left. These six stages should be repeated together three to seven times. We can imagine the energy from within us rising to our third eye or the center of our forehead. Once we complete the breathing exercise, it's a perfect opportunity to just listen to the silence, breathing in and breathing out.

When we do our centering exercise daily, we will begin to notice a transformation taking place in our consciousness. We will begin to realize that what holds us all together is not merely the air, or the invisible ethers of consciousness – not just the pulsation of light and earth – but a force that is even more dynamic. When we surrender to this force, we will feel all of the worries, all of the concerns, all of the cares, all of the reactions that we had to the world around us just disappear. We will begin to feel a surge of peace and share a oneness or connection with everything and everyone in a manner that is greater than the circumstances in the material world. We will begin to feel the power of this force everywhere present but most importantly as part of us. If we relax and let go, we can feel it emanating from the bottom of our feet to the top of our head. We will begin to feel the magnitude of this force from the innermost depths of our being. We will begin to feel an inner radiance that shines through us simply because we realize that we are beings of light – full of unlimited possibility. This force will strengthen us with the understanding that nothing and no one can stop us from achieving our greatest good.

Regardless of what activity we do, whether it be practicing law, body-building, writing books, or teaching classes, there must be resting periods, when we cease all outer activity and tap into the universe so that we begin to develop a connection to unlimited source, to that unlimited well of divine ideas that will give us what we need when we need it. In our humanness, there is a limit to what we can do. But in the Spirit, we connect with a greater power than us – a universe that will facilitate the divine appointments, open the closed doors, find the desired partners, manifest the right resources, tie the loose ends, and make ways out of no way – to do for us what we could never do for ourselves.

AFFIRMATION FOR CENTERING

I center in the power in which I live and move and have my being.

*I center in the flow of inexhaustible supply
and the energy of endless possibilities.*

*I center in infinite source, trusting that the universe
is always blessing me, always anointing me,
always prospering me, always protecting me.*

*I center in the consciousness of perfect divine order,
knowing that the universe can do its work without me.*

*I center in the invisible ethers that are attracting the right people,
the right circumstances, and the right situations
that will manifest my greatest dreams.*

*I center in the divine mind that connects us all as one,
knowing that even in the unseen –
the universe is conspiring to help me
attain my goals and that all of my good is taking shape.*

center in the joy of letting go and letting success express through me.

ACCOUNTABILITY PARTNER/S

_____
_____
_____
_____

HOW DO WE LISTEN?   MEDITATION ON THE BREATH OF LIFE

_____
_____
_____
_____
_____
_____
_____
_____
_____
_____
_____

HOW DO WE RECEIVE? MEDITATION ON OLDER SELF

_____
_____
_____
_____
_____
_____
_____
_____
_____
_____
_____
_____

HOW DO WE STAY CONNECTED? MEDITATION ON THE KINGDOM WITHIN

_____
_____
_____
_____
_____
_____
_____
_____
_____
_____

4 THE LAW OF TELLING A NEW STORY

"That is why," Dale said, "it is so important for people to release the old worn-out excuses and lies they've told themselves, the resentments they've conjured up to hide their fears, and the habits they've latched on to just so they won't have to step up to the plate and take responsibility for themselves. The only way to move beyond the pity parties and the energy drained from complaining is to tell a new story. A new story is the co-creative energy of the universe which gives way to a new perception of the experience in which we live." Najih liked the concept of viewing his life as the story that he was telling. It gave him a more global sense of control: it was his story; he was calling the shots; it could begin, develop, soar, resolve, climax, and end the way that he wanted.

What if the story that we told ourselves was not about the past, not about the mistakes that we made – not about something we did wrong or how someone wronged us? What if the only thing that we focused on was that we are and always have been in the safekeeping of absolute good? What if the only thing we focused on was the creation of something brand new in us – something that aligned itself with the universe from the now moment going forward?

We have to start accepting the fact that all of the good, all of the love, all of the wealth, all of the beauty, all of the gratitude, all of the recognition, all of the success is already within us. We have to close the chapter to our past and dare to write a new story, a powerful story, a story of unlimited resources, a story overflowing with divine ideas, a story that stops us from being a spiritual captive in somebody else's melodrama, a story in which we freely leave the nets that we have been hanging onto for so long, a story that gives us the alignment with our greatness by re-dedicating our lives to the good that only we desire.

This means that we have to stop dancing to somebody else's tune, start singing our own song, writing our own lyrics, and starring in our own script. Our story should be told in a new way, in a manner that does not diminish who we are or any aspect of our divine inheritance. Our new story cannot be a story of pity. In fact, from this moment forth, we cannot entertain a single pity party. It's not a story of refuge. It's not a story of wallowing in hopelessness or sifting through someone else's turmoil. It is a story of power, our power as a child of the universe. We must dedicate ourselves right now to stop telling the story of sorrow, poverty, disappointment, and despair. We must stop telling the story of fear. We must stop telling the story of what he did, she did, they did or didn't do because the universe is limitless and there are endless ways for good to take shape. We must dedicate ourselves right now to a new story – starring every hope, every dream, every desire, every pre-paving prayer that we can utter. We have to dedicate ourselves to a story of greatness that has never been told before – one in which we accomplish every dream that we ever had and more, a story where we receive the appropriate recognition, a story where we receive a standing ovation, a story where best picture is just one of many rewards.

When our new story unfolds, nothing and no one can prevent the goodness, abundance and the divine ideas that will change our lives forever. As our new story unfolds, we will have the triumph of a victory that is everlasting. We need to tell a new story of being smart enough, good-looking enough, creative enough, loving enough, and nurturing enough. We need to tell a new story, one where we stop cheating ourselves, limiting ourselves and doubting ourselves. We need to tell a new story of not second-guessing our infinite abilities, not doing less than what the universe called us to do, not interrupting the endless creative flow of good that the universe is pouring into our life. We have to move ourselves out of the way so that the blessings that the universe has in store for us will manifest quickly. We have to stop yearning for one thing in our heart but another thing in our actions. We have to stop just going through the motions in our lives, living that nagging sensation of unhappiness – because we are cheating ourselves by living a lie.

We have to tell a new story by leaving any situation that is not for our highest good. We have to be faithful to the dreams that the universe has given us – and not let anything or anyone undermine them. We have to stop doubting that we can accomplish our goals. If anything or anyone gets in the way of our higher good and our greatest purpose, we have to cast them away, and stop cheating ourselves. We are divine creation – put here for a purpose.

CHAPTER ONE:

_____

Once upon a time, a little _____ was born to

_____

_____

The first thing that _____ remembers is

_____

_____

_____

By the time_____ was

_____ years old,

_____

_____

_____

The best thing that _____ ever experienced as a child was

_____

_____

_____

_____

_____

_____On _____day,

_____ fell down when

_____

_____

_____

_____was locked

inside a dungeon when

_____

_____

_____

CHAPTER TWO: _____

The following people are the main characters of
_____'s story. They were always available to promote,
push, pull, and deliver in the following ways:

_____
_____
_____
_____

_____ fought until realizing that:

_____
_____
_____
_____

_____ had to climb a hill of:

_____
_____
_____
_____

_____ had to swim through a river of:

_____
_____
_____
_____
_____

_____ had to lift:

_____
_____
_____

had to dig deep within, so s/he could find her/his true intention:_____

_____

_____

_____

_____ and with that understanding, s/he suddenly found her/himself enlightened,

_____

_____

_____

_____

_____

_____and through that enlightenment – became freed.

CHAPTER THREE:

_____

_____ became a:

_____

_____

_____

_____

_____

_____

_____ appeared:

_____

_____

_____

_____

_____ spread wings and flew beyond:

_____
_____
_____

_____ discovered a world inside that was:

_____
_____
_____
_____
_____
_____

_____ was overjoyed because:

_____
_____
_____
_____
_____

In this new story, _____ realized that:

_____
_____
_____
_____
_____
_____

AFFIRMATION OF TELLING A NEW STORY

Today is a new day, now is a new moment.

Today I release the past.

Today I release any and everyone who I thought was standing in my way.

Today I forgive myself for what I didn't do. And I forgive myself for what I did.

I forgive myself for the mistakes I made.

I forgive myself for the strength I lacked.

I forgive myself for the goals I have not yet accomplished.

I forgive myself for not doing what I had hoped to do.

I forgive myself for not being forgiving.

Today, I put away the old, and I welcome the new.

I'm not carrying any more of my baggage or any baggage for anyone else.

The only thing I'm bringing is so much good, so much joy, so much love, so much abundance, so much success, so much wisdom – I cannot even begin to imagine it!

The only consciousness I'm bringing is one steeped in unlimited source, infinite possibility, and inexhaustible supply!

In my new story, I move outside of the confines of fear, outside the confines of lack, outside the confines of self-imposed restrictions, and I get in synch with the pure potential of the universe that is restoring me, recreating me, redefining me, and resurrecting me with miracles well beyond the realm of my expectations.

In my new story, I step into my greatness, which is the fullest expression of everything that I am.

I become the person I was meant to be.

In my new story, I release anything less than the fullest expression of everything that I AM.

I'm going to dance on the edge of pure potential right now.

I'm going to fly with the wings of new hope right now.

I'm going to step into my greatness right now.

I'm going to co-create with the miraculous power that I am right now.

I can feel it in my bones right now.

I have awakened from my sleep right now.

I'm going to stop resisting right now.

I'm going through the open door right now.

I'm going to move with unlimited love in my heart right now.

In my new story, my dreams are unfolding. In my new story, my prayers are being answered.

In my new story, my house is in order. In my new story, my ideas have taken root.

In my new story, my body is cleansed with perfect health and healing.

In my new story, my good is here in the midst of infinite blessings.

In my new story, I am victorious. In my new story, my goals are reached.

In my new story, I stand on the shoulders of faith.

In my new story, I stop hesitating and complaining and blaming.

This is the year of the manifestation of my dreams.

I see them manifesting with the consciousness of a new glory.

5 THE LAW OF CREATING OPPORTUNITY

"Every mistake is an opportunity," Dale had just said the previous morning . . . . "Every challenge is an opportunity. Every failure is an opportunity. Every firing or downsizing is an opportunity. We just have to bless the situation and move on. People think that messiness and disarray and mistakes are not part of success but they are because without them, we would never grow."

We create opportunity when we are clear about what we want to succeed in doing.

No one can determine what we are called to do but us, and even we have to listen deeply to discern our true calling. When we know what we want to do, we attract even more opportunities because we are better able to communicate what we want to others. We are better able to move in the direction of our dreams. Ironically, people are interested in helping people who help themselves. Moreover, we exude more confidence when we are headed in the right direction. Clarity pushes open the right doors because we bring the right motivation and momentum to move them.

We create opportunity when we build relationships.

If we want to network, then we can start by looking in our immediate environment – in our classrooms, communities and workplaces. The people we know and love right now are the ones who may ultimately make a difference in our lives. We have to start by being credible, responsible and reliable with our classmates, colleagues and acquaintances because that is where our reputation begins. We never know which one of our relationships will bring us the most opportunities. Oftentimes, the least-expected people bring the most blessings.

The best way to network is by keeping in touch with and getting to know people in the profession who are similar to us but also those who are different. We never know where our good is coming from. Moreover, we never know how we may be able to help other people. In addition to mentors, it's also good to have a few people in our corner to keep us on track – someone like our spouse, who doesn't allow us to stop short of our goals. We need someone who doesn't judge us when we make mistakes but helps us figure out a way to learn from them and maximize our potential. These people, who are just close friends in our corner, are our accountability partners – just like a workout partner; we help keep each other on track.

We create opportunity when we step outside of our boxes.

We have to be willing to step outside of the known and venture into the unknown. We cannot limit ourselves. We cannot be shy about seeking what we want out of life. We cannot dwell on the appearances of lack and limitation. Otherwise, we will lose before we get started. We have to push ourselves outside of our comfort zones to experience the fullest extent of our hopes, dreams and aspirations.

We create opportunity through forgiveness.

We cannot be effective if we are hanging on to grudges and resentments against anyone – our adversaries, colleagues, friends, or associates – regardless of what has happened. We cannot move forward if we are holding onto the past. By letting go of negativity and toxic energy in our relationships, we can release the past and refrain from burning any bridges. Oftentimes, the person who we believe is our enemy blesses us with the most good. Even if the person doesn't bless us, we block the flow of God's channels when we give them our energy. The goal is to release the past and move forward freely.

We create opportunity through a presence that is conscientious and compassionate.

We have to master being courteous, respectful, thoughtful, and kind. This doesn't require that we be pretentious or different than who we really are, but it does require that we be gracious despite our own challenges. We sometimes have to bite our tongues and say less; speak up and say more; go the extra mile to work harder; or bend over backwards to be patient – in order to be conscientious and compassionate. This means that we have to look people in their eyes when we speak to them, as well as when they are speaking. We must have firm handshakes. We must be active listeners. We should remember names. We should be sensitive to body language. We should stay abreast of the current events in our profession. We should stay in touch with cards, email messages, telephone calls, and visits.

We create opportunity by maintaining a professional online presence.

Today's social media requires that we be visible and professional on Facebook, Linked-In, Twitter, and other website communities that will help us further our professional contacts. The ease with which we can create blogs and websites encourages us to blog on the issues that would support our profession, business or calling. Everything that we do is part of our professional brand, so we have to be careful, always rise about the fray, and always be positive in our online presence. Technology creates opportunity. We have to develop our tech skills and not be afraid to use the technological vehicles that will help us. Some of the recent technological innovations can be found on mashable.com, fastcompany.com, and wired.com.

We create opportunity by joining professional and trade organizations.

Once we join professional groups, we can do more productive networking by giving our time to one or more of their committees. We can also go to national professional conferences and related meetings of trade organizations. We have to know the top people in the field that we are interested in; the firms that are out there; and the people who at least have our level of experience. A lot of professional organizations hold events that allow volunteers to attend for free, if cost is an issue. It is important to note that organizations take on the personality of their leadership. We are the future leaders, so we have to bring the voice and the insight and the goals that we would like to contribute.

We create opportunity when we give.

We all have something to offer regardless of the amount of professional experience we have. Some of the greatest things that we can give are encouragement, respect, courtesy, compassion, understanding, and patience. These gifts, which are free, mean a great deal to people and thus result in a great deal of good flowing back in return. Everyone should be given these gifts – regardless of their station in life: the delivery man, the maintenance woman, the receptionist, the secretary, the mail clerk, even an adversary, should be treated just as kindly and professionally as the chief executive officer, president, vice president or client. We give when we are reliable, disciplined, dependable, and willing to put forth more than the concerted effort. We create opportunity when we are charitable because we always receive what we give. We reap what we sow. When we give of our time, our skills and our talent, we give to ourselves because we learn more, demonstrate more, and experience more.

We create opportunity when we are grateful.

Gratitude is not something that we should do just to make others feel good. Gratitude creates opportunity because it brings the energy of joy, appreciation and abundance. Gratitude is akin to fertilizer when it comes to success; it strengthens, builds, fortifies, and helps success grow. The more thanks we give, the more blessings we receive. The more appreciation we give, the more people are willing to do for us.

MASTER MIND GROUPS

In his best-selling book Think and Grow Rich, *Napoleon Hill encouraged everyone to use the "Power of the Master Mind" through "coordination of knowledge and effort, in a spirit of harmony, between two or more people, for the attainment of a definite purpose."*

Master Mind Principle One:

I accept all of the good that the universe has in store for me. [Discuss and note three ways that you can accept the good that the universe has in store for you.]

1. _____

2. _____

3. _____

Master Mind Principle Two:

I receive the answer that I have been looking for. [Discuss and note three answers that you are given to three questions, desires, goals that you need answering.]

1. _____

2. _____

3. _____

Master Mind Principle Three: I move beyond what I used to be into what I am.
[Discuss and note three ways that you are prepared to change.]

1. _____

2. _____

3. _____

Master Mind Principle Four: I realize my divine connection to the inexhaustible source of the universe. [Discuss and note three ways that you can realize the power of God or whatever you want to call the Divine.]

1. _____

2. _____

3. _____

Master Mind Principle Five: I let go of the past. [Discuss and note three people, situations, thoughts or habits that you will release.]

1. _____

2. _____

3. _____

Master Mind Principle Six: I ask, and I receive. [Discuss three things that you really want but never really thought you would receive.]

1. _____

2. _____

3. _____

Master Mind Principle Seven: I am grateful – or great-filled – because I know that I have been blessed. [Discuss three things that you are grateful for.]

1. _____

2. _____

3. _____

Master Mind Principle Eight: I serve others. [Discuss three ways that you will utilize what you desire doing to benefit others.]

1. _____

2. _____

3. _____

LIST CONTACT INFORMATION, A GOAL FOR EACH MEMBER, INITIAL THOUGHTS ON WHAT EACH PERSON CAN DO TO CREATE OPPORTUNITY, THOSE YOU KNOW WHO MIGHT BE HELPFUL TO THEM, WHAT YOU PERSONALLY CAN BRING TO THE PICTURE.

_____
_____
_____
_____
_____
_____
_____
_____
_____
_____
_____
_____
_____
_____
_____
_____
_____

AFFIRMATION FOR CREATING OPPORTUNITY

I create the opportunities that I need to succeed.
In creating new opportunities, I don't worry
about what others may say or think.
In creating new opportunities, I move myself out of the way.
In creating new opportunities, I demonstrate
that I have unique gifts and talents
so that I can manifest the good work
that I was created to do.
In creating new opportunities, I create my goals
and I make them the priority.
In creating new opportunities, I stop asking
what the future has in store for me,
and instead affirm what I have in store for the future.
In creating new opportunities, I do the research
and I am guided into places
that I never could have imagined.
In creating new opportunities, I turn on and
tune into the absolute good of the universe
– and I am blessed.
In creating new opportunities, I use the power of gratitude,
and I say thanks –
realizing that once I plant my seeds of success,
success immediately begins taking root
through the challenges and mistakes
and failures that once made me feel inadequate.
I now realize that they were stepping stones.

6 THE LAW OF SPEAKING TRUTH TO POWER

"Our voices," Dale began, "are meant to be heard.
We have within us a power that takes shape when spoken words are formed in the ethers.
We all have the ability to speak truth to power.
What I mean by that is that we can say something and then those words
immediately begin to shape and form and materialize exactly what we want....
You think that you are just talking or chatting
or commiserating in some self-inflicted pity party —
but meanwhile you are co-creating with whatever comes out of your mouth."

Dale was more adamant than Najih had ever seen him.

Dale looked directly at Yashita as he was speaking.
"Of course people want you to shut up.
Of course they don't want you to be heard.
Of course they want to silence you because your voice is your power.
You stand in the front of a jury or a judge and you are bringing about change.
You are power and you stand in one of the most powerful vehicles in this society —
the halls of justice where man-made laws are changed
and altered and fixed and solidified and modified and divined —
and there you are representing in so many different ways.
There you are speaking truth to power with a voice that is pure because it has never been silenced before."

Every single thought, every word, every single utterance is speaking truth to power, so we have to watch what we say. We cannot speak in a manner that undermines our greatness. We cannot marginalize the success that we are. We cannot utter that we're not good enough because we are better than the best. There is nothing and no one for us to fear — especially a bully because they are the most afraid of all. All we have to do is what we need to do and keep on stepping. We need to turn off the monologues that doubt us — that frustrate our potential — that worry about what someone else says or thinks or does — that are stuck in the past — that are worrying about the future. We cannot minimize the good that comes with saying great things about ourselves. We are special; we are unique; we are divine. We should expect the best. Success is blessing us right now.

We will have to give an account on judgment day for every careless word that we utter. But we have to realize when judgment day is: it's every day. We die daily, but wake up in the kingdom of success to continue on our journey. It's the period of reaping what we sow in thought, word and action. We do that every day. We cannot hide under the covers of worry and speak failure, dwelling on how everything is screwed up for us, or someone wasn't nice to us or how so and so is not treating us fairly. When we dwell in the past, we fail to lift up the power of who we are. When we keep talking about the negative, we give power to it.

If we talk about being poor, then we decree poverty. If we talk about illness, we decree it. If we talk about bad relationships, we decree them. If we talk about insecurity, or loneliness, or lack, we decree it. We have to shift the paradigm and instead of wallowing in it; we have to step up to the plate and begin affirming how we are going to use our lives and invest our resources to change it.

AFFIRMATION OF SPEAKING TRUTH TO POWER

I speak truth to power. The words and thoughts that I speak plant seeds into the universal soil of energy; opening doors and avenues and opportunities to receive all that I desire.

I speak truth to power. I know that if I want to experience success in my life, I have to be successful within my own consciousness: loving and compassionate and understanding and honest. I have to speak the words to myself that allow me to become that which I seek in success.

I speak truth to power. If I want prosperity in my life, I have to be prosperous in my own consciousness: I have to ask the universe for what I want, and since it is so, I just have to claim it.

This is my season. This is my time to speak truth to power! This is my time to acknowledge the greatness within.

I speak truth to power.

My table is prepared before my enemies. My battle is won. My mustard seed has grown.
My water is walked. My vision is restored.

This is my season.
My peace is stilled. What I asked is answered. Where I knocked is opened.
Where I sought has found.

This is my season.
I soar in its Everlasting Power. I fly in its Infinite Possibility. I dance in its Perfect Harmony.
I leap in its Joyful Success.

This is my season because I know that Spirit is moving through my life.
I am one with the omnipotence, omniscience and omnipresence of Success.

Everything is in perfect divine order.
Whatever I need, whatever I long for is manifesting when it is supposed to.
I am in my right place at my right time.
Manna feeds me success every day.

The time to move away from appearances is now.
The time to move away from confusion is now.
The time to move forward as a full expression of all that success is – is now.

WRITING YOUR AFFIRMATION

There is no set way to write an affirmation, but certain rules will help provide a better understanding of what they are, as well as the basics regarding how they should be structured. If you follow these guidelines to write your own affirmations and create empowering statements, there is no question that you will see the manifestation of your success from speaking them with power, boldness and courage.

- **Be personal.** Use "I," "me," and or your first name.

- **Begin with denials.** Denials are assertions of what is not going to take place in your life, what will not harm you. For example, "no one and nothing can keep my good from me" is a denial. It is believed that the universe abhors a vacuum, so denials clean out the undesirable thoughts and energy and affirmations fill consciousness with the new.

- **Be positive.** Affirm what you want as if your good has already manifested, as if your prayers have already been answered.

- **Use the present tense.** Speak as though what you speak has already taken place, e.g., : **"I am." " I have." "I can."** The universe does not know time. The good that you seek has already taken shape. For example, you can say "I have the perfect, divine job." Or "I passed the Bar with a score high enough to waive into the DC Bar."

- **Use action words.** E.g., "I accomplish my good with ease." "My cup runs over." "God is blessing me right now." "I drive my new Mercedes with joy."

- **Set aside time each day and practice repeating your affirmations beginning each morning and throughout the day. Recite the affirmation out loud four times.** When you say affirmations to get what you want, you have to say them over and over until your subconscious mind acts upon them.

- **Feel and connect with the emotion you would have when receiving what you speak.** Your consciousness responds to what you desire when saying affirmations with intent and purpose, knowing and satisfaction.

- **Never limit your desires.** Let the power of your heart, mind and soul reach for the stars. If you dream of one day becoming President, for example, you could affirm: **"I am proud as I stand in the White House meeting with my Cabinet."**

- **Recite your affirmations daily.** Speak truth to power each day, preferably in the morning, by reciting your entire affirmation four times out loud. If you have time, follow with a meditation.

- **Envision what you speak.** Close your eyes and see the images described and believe it is so.

Practice writing affirmations as follows:

I am one with Success, therefore, I AM:

_____
_____
_____
_____

I release everyone who has harmed me, realizing that no one and nothing can keep me from my greatest good. I release and forgive:

_____
_____
_____

I have everything that I need, including:

_____
_____
_____
_____

My life is a perfect reflection of the Absolute Good, so I:

_____
_____
_____
_____
_____

My blessings keep pouring, streaming, flowing over, in so many different ways:

_____
_____
_____
_____
_____
_____
_____
_____
_____
_____
_____
_____
_____
_____
_____
_____
_____

SPEAKING TRUTH TO POWER

7 THE LAW OF SEEING ABSOLUTE GOOD

"Well, I can see success some of the time," Olga said, pretending to be a student with questions, "and then the other times, I can worry and be miserable about the good that my neighbor has – as if it would take something from me. I can spend an hour trusting the divine and then the rest of the time, I can forget that the power is within me and instead believe that what my neighbor has is what I need – not realizing that my calling is different. I can talk the talk about the universe being good, but I cannot walk the walk without fear and self-limitation."

She and Dale were pretending to be at the opposite ends of the spectrum of faith.

Dale chimed in – "But, oh, if I seek first the Kingdom of Absolute Good – if I open my inner eye of imagination and envision the good in me waiting to express through me, I realize I can succeed."

We can create and envision something greater than what we can see, touch and feel. Our difficulties arise when we believe that we are separate from the power that the universe gives us. We have to stay consistent and centered in the greatness of Success's bounty – through meditation, affirmation, and prayer. When we are centered, we attract the right people, circumstances, opportunities, and the divine ideas to bless us.

Our creative vision allows us to create good for not only ourselves but to be a constant blessing, inspiration, and resource to others. Vision always leads us to the pasture of opportunity – if we see rightly. If we need a teacher, the teacher appears. If we need a client, the client shows up. If we need an answer, it is given. If we need discernment, the right decision guides us through what we need to do. No matter what we are up against, no matter what the appearances look like, no matter what the threat – it better beware because success is with us: the Good Shepherd, the Infinite Power, the Almighty One who says that the battle is mine, the One who says touch not my anointed and do my prophets no harm, and the One who teaches us that all we have to do is believe.

Our weapon is our faith. When we are tapped in, turned on, and connected with source, all the traffic lights turn green in our favor; the train arrives as soon as we walk to the platform; unexpected money arrives. The right person shows up at the right time, and says I will do this for you. The right doors just open. The wall or barrier that was blocking our good is removed, and the way out of no way becomes the path to endless possibilities. We will be blessed from the top of our head to the bottom of our feet. Our good will flow from so many different directions that we cannot even begin to imagine what will be in store for us. The highways and the byways will just pour, rain down blessings on us. There is nothing that we need. All of our desires are fulfilled. We have everything that we want. But we have to open our gift of imagination and see our good for ourselves.

There is no need to misappropriate or interfere with something belonging to someone else. If we are centered, we realize that we don't need what we have because the universe is always blessing us with our highest good. We stop dwelling in a mentality of wanting because the universe supplies our every need. We begin to cultivate a consciousness which realizes that there is nothing that we cannot do and nothing that we cannot have because there is a power in us that attracts what we need before we even ask.

We have to envision boldly. We cannot limit our visions to what we see before us. We have to be visionary enough to see its full potential. We have to envision the best for our growth, our economy's improvement, our judicial system's integrity. We have to stretch beyond our the confines of our frustration to contribute. We have to see our financial institutions, government and leaders strengthened, sustained and enlightened. We have to see good for those around us; see ourselves standing with our feet on solid ground. We have to see unlimited source all around us. We have to see a success that has no reserve, no budget, and no limit.

We have the ability to see, imagine and envision what the universe calls us to co-create. The more that we tap into, tune in, and turn on absolute good, we know exactly what we are called to do. The universe will unfold how we can accomplish our goals and put the right people and circumstances in our lives to help us. But we have to start by at least envisioning our success. There are a million ways to envision our success – to center and believe in what we want so deeply that we become open and receptive to the manifestation of our desires. Here are a few that definitely work.

Morning Stillness Meditation – Do not ask for anything or say anything, just sit quietly in the stillness for 5, 10, 15 minutes or more. This allows us to center ourselves in our highest consciousness – so that we can receive the vision that the universe is giving us. This will bless us profoundly. It may not seem like much at all, but centering in the stillness is the most powerful meditation that we can have. Once we tune into the universe, what we need to know to accomplish our good will be revealed. This works great with goal setting: when we know what our goals are, silent meditation in the stillness will open up ways to allow them to take shape.

In addition to doing a meditation in the silence, stillness of the mind can also be achieved by centering in music. We all have our favorite music that immediately centers us and moves our consciousness to a level that transcends the physical plane and removes the distractions of the day to the realization that there is something greater than who we are in the physical realm. Gospel, New Age, Pop, Soul – anything can be used that helps us feel one with the universe.

Morning Affirmation – Another powerful way to envision success is to focus on what we want in our lives and write these desires out as if they have already happened – thanking the universe for them. It is important to also include at the beginning some general affirmations to establish our center in consciousness, such as repeating "I AM"; "I AM THAT I AM"; "I AM One with Spirit"; "I AM One with Inexhaustible Source"; "I AM One with Unlimited Supply"; "I live and move and have my being in God"; "I ask and I receive." Release anything that is bothering you, as if it is gone (*e.g.*, I AM Whole and Healed; Nothing and no one can keep me from attaining my greatest good). Add goals, dreams, wishes, needs, desires in as many affirmative sentences as necessary (*e.g.*, I AM an all A student; I receive the title as Chief Judge; I publish my book). End the affirmation by gratitude and affirming that God will bless you with your greatest success above and beyond what you could ever imagine. Repeat your full affirmation aloud at least three times. Each time that you repeat it, envision it, see it, claim it. And at the end, sit quietly in the presence.

Projected Diary – The concept of the projected diary is taken from Eric Butterworth's book, *The Creative Life*. It requires writing in a journal either at night or in the morning – as if the day has already passed and visualize exactly how it should play out – only seeing the good of course. Either our good will take shape immediately or we will begin the process of the manifestation of our good in the universe over time. The seeds will be planted.

Evening Visualization – When we go to bed at night, we can envision what we want to do by seeing ourselves accomplishing it. This, too, will transform our lives and open our consciousness to the unlimited potential that we are. This works especially well when fear is blocking us from manifesting what we have been called to do. The truth is that there is no end to the blessings that the universe can pour into our lives. As visionaries, we should not be limited by fear, which blinds us to what we can accomplish.

TREASURE MAP

THIS IS A PICTURE OF WHAT I DESIRE IN MY LIFE

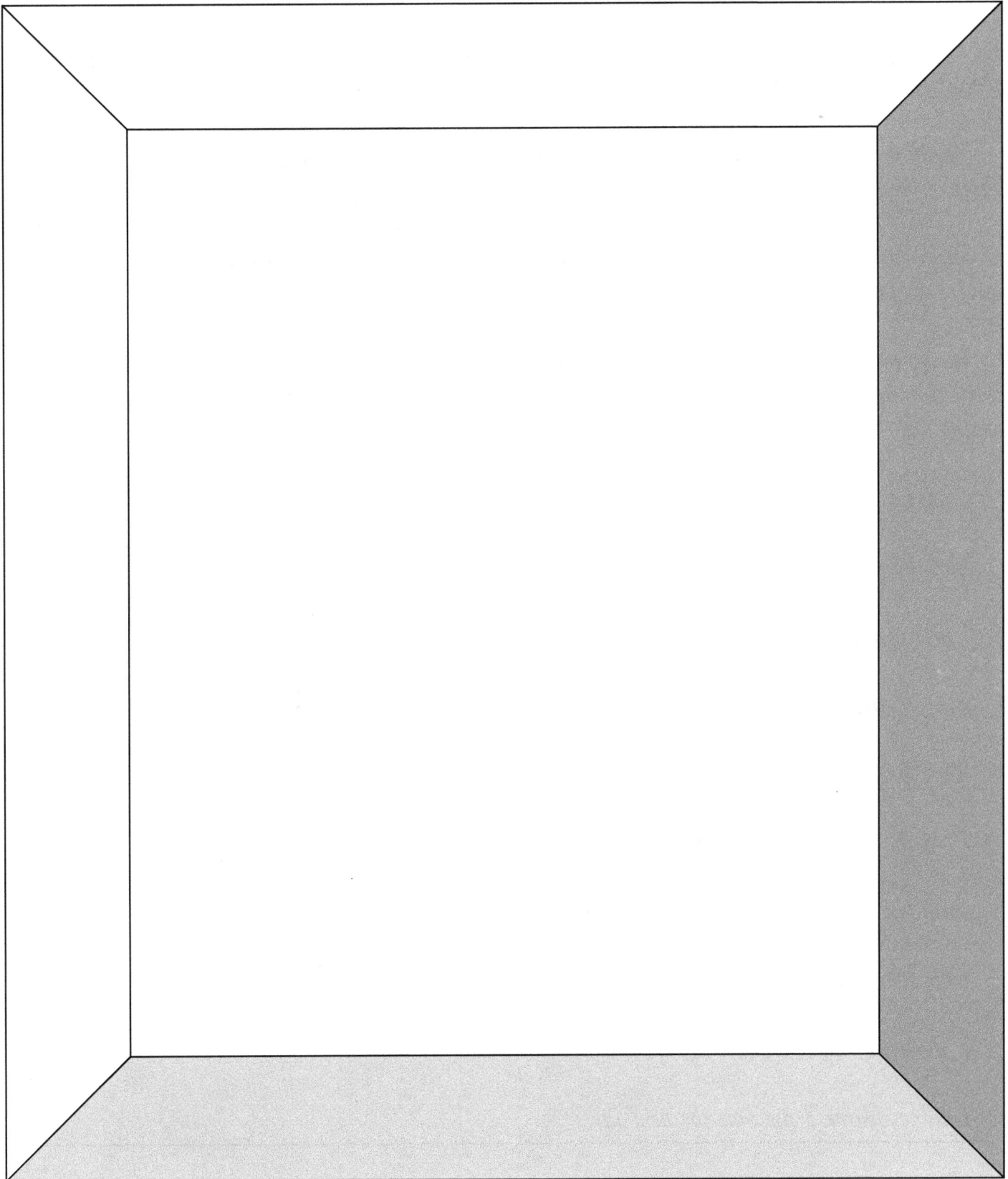

Affirmation of Seeing Absolute Good

I have a new vision.

In my new vision, I am embraced by absolute good in everything that I do, in every place where I go, through every person who I meet.

In my new vision, I am the creative expression of the universe, multiplying two fish and five loaves of bread, enlarging my territory, and realizing that these and greater things shall I do.

In my new vision, the universe is my only refuge, my highest consciousness, my habitation of prayer, my home of meditation, my hope of glory.

In my new vision, unlimited potential carries me through the waves of this storm of reform, restructure and rebirth — knowing that soon I will begin to see the changes that I have been longing for.

I seize now the courage that I have awaited.

I shake now the dust off my shoes.

I move on the path of righteousness.

Angels take charge over me.

They keep me in all Success's ways. They lift me up in their hands.

I am the manifestation of absolute good that I see.

And yet, I wear humility like the strength that it is.

I do the work that I am blessed to do.

I am not afraid because I am a seer.

I do not worry. I welcome the new day.

8 THE LAW OF SHINING OUR LIGHT

> *"We all have an inner light of radiance. It shines through every aspect of our being. The third eye is said to connect us with the universe, so the light of the body is said to be illuminated through the third eye," Dale said. "The Scripture says if therefore our eye be single, meaning single and focused in absolute good, then our whole body — meaning our entire being — shall be full of light. The ability to be one with higher consciousness — that is to be fully connected with our light — is what this journey in life is all about. If we do not stay consistent with our studies and centering in the truth, we remain vulnerable to situations that don't go the way we want them to; to the mishaps along the path that we thought was free of obstacles. There will always be obstacles, but nothing interferes with the light."*

Shining our lights requires that we be liberated from the feelings, doubts, expectations of others — and do what we were called to do. We cannot, however, shine our light in all of its brilliance if we are distracted by other things. It goes without saying that we have to rise above pettiness and signifying — the negative vibrations of other people. We also have to rise above the appearances of things that we expected to go a certain way. When things don't go our perceived way, it is because the universe has something better in store. Don't forget that we are not limited by the physical.

We have at our disposal the omnipotent spiritual realm, so we shouldn't limit ourselves to what we can see in the flesh. We must keep our eyes single and focused on absolute good. If we entertain anything less, we will create it for ourselves. If our eye is not single, we are more likely to multiply our errors, lose our perspective, and do foolish things. We are more likely to say things we later regret. We are more likely to waste time that could have been well spent. We are more likely to act out of negative emotions rather than with confidence and purpose. When we fail to keep our focus on a higher consciousness rather than the fleeting rewards of the flesh, we will find ourselves in the dark, with our inner light off — blinded by our lack of faith. Faith is what gives us power. Faith is what makes us prosper. Faith is what makes us whole. Faith is what makes our lights shine their brightest.

If our eye is single, our whole body shall be full of light. But if we are not centered daily in the light within, our direction, our intuition, our divine compass turns off, and we will end up stumbling in darkness. The scales will not fall from our eyes until we begin to see through the appearances of things. If we fail to quiet ourselves enough to listen, then our focus will be scattered, and we will bang into walls created from our spiritual blindness. Silence and stillness gives way to the light that unifies us in consciousness and centers us in our divine nature.

When someone says "let there be light," it means let there be light present in its entirety at the point at which we are: that is the inner light which guides our entire being. Our third eye is that inner eye that we see from when we meditate, when we practice looking within, when we are filled with the light emanating from the cosmic vibration of wisdom that informs all beings. When we center in this divine light, we open our spiritual eye, our inner eye, our third eye to the presence of absolute good, and our entire being is filled with light. It is in this consciousness that we stay focused.

Work is more than just a job — it is about giving our best to the world. As long as we perceive our work as a job, we will never be happy. Shining our lights means that we are not simply doing the best that we can do — we are building our lives and establishing our careers, which is much more significant than just a job. Not having a job does not prevent us from improving our understanding of our field, by attending courses outside our employment in areas that support our practice, our expertise and our interest. We must develop a library of articles, training memoranda, books and other resources that will serve us no matter where we practice. We must become active in our professional communities, as well as improve our professional development and our ability to contribute to the legal community. We must volunteer on pro bono matters so that we can contribute to those in need. We must give time and energy to ourselves, our family, our church, and our hobbies.

These days, the least-traveled road is the road where one takes responsibility for one's life — as opposed to expecting someone else to provide meaningful opportunities; the road where one doesn't wait for the world to deliver work but rises up to provide service; the road where one doesn't limit their contribution based on a level of experience – but gives their best no matter what; the road where one respects everyone – regardless of their station; the road where one doesn't hide behind merely providing assistance but finds ways to contribute to the big picture; the road where one doesn't limit oneself to whatever one knows but excels in researching and understanding the background of every potential relevant substantive issue and possible procedural posture.

It's amazing how many young lawyers work on an assignment and fail to do any background research. One can quickly acquire a workable overview of the law applicable to any subject by researching the area. It may be the first complaint or discovery request drafted; the first merger, antitrust, securities, false advertising, or products liability matter worked on; the first expert witness interviewed; the first contract drafted; the first due diligence assignment given; the first deposition taken; or the first trial – but that does not mean we should remain ignorant. It is a perfect opportunity to review a treatise, handbook, outline, law review article, internet material, or other resources and learn as much as we can about the area – increasing our knowledge each time we have a task.

We owe it to everyone – not just to ourselves – to experience absolute good, which means realizing why we are here on this planet, at this time and place. Our decision to be successful puts us on the least traveled road. It's so much easier to be mediocre; to do less than our best; to sleep late and get entangled in so much foolishness at night that we lose perspective about what we should be doing. Do we want to be extraordinary or common? Do we want to change our life or keep doing the same old same old? Are we going to take responsibility for what we fail to do for ourselves, and stop blaming other people and stop lying to ourselves about what everyone else is doing to us? Are we courageous enough, wise enough, worthy enough to leave our comfort zones and discover who we really are? Are we bold enough to be inventive enough to transform our life and begin to be the change that we want to see in the world?

Seven Steps of Light

Discuss How to Embrace the Light

We have to let our lights shine simply by being our true selves, that which makes us utterly and uniquely us, that place in which we truly connect with and become enlightened as an individual creative expression of the universe.

We have to listen to the small, still voice within, the drive within us to express that which is so magnificent that its light *will* ultimately shine through our need to do what's safe; our need to stay within the box; our need to conform.

Our inner light will ultimately force us to listen – not to degrees and stature and material things – but to the unique calling of who we are. We are saved – not when we hold back – but when we dare to trust the universe enough to boldly and courageously be the person who we have been most afraid of becoming.

Walking in the light means walking in the divine ethers that we were born into – the ethers of infinite substance and creative visions and everlasting dreams – without caring about what others think.

Embracing the light means that we have to let go of anything that may be clouding our vision. What is standing in your way?

_____
_____
_____
_____
_____
_____
_____
_____
_____
_____

Discuss How to Prophesy Success

We do not have to go to fortune tellers because we have the power to prophesy our own good — to think it; to believe it; to claim it; and to see it. When we believe, we don't worry about what we don't see; and we don't worry about what we do see. But we can co-create our good because we are best able to discern what we desire.

We co-create by decreeing our good. We must speak the truth — that God-Source-Power will pour so many blessings upon us, we will not have space enough to receive them. Life is an echo; it always returns the call sent out. The spoken word is the first projection of creative mind into the realm of form; manifestation always follows.

Discuss how to let the light shine through words, communications, voice, writings, etc.

_____
_____
_____
_____
_____
_____
_____
_____
_____
_____
_____
_____
_____
_____

Discuss Your Game Plan for Success

In order to co-create our good, we must choose it, list it, decide it, design it, plan it. When we are clear about what we want, the Spirit expressing as us will work through the unlimited greatness of all that it is to unfold for us unlimited substance.

Spirit draws to us whatever we need for its manifestation. **Our good unfolds when we write out our goals for the DAY, the WEEK, the MONTH, the YEAR, and the next FIVE YEARS – and study them daily. Write it out; write it out; write it out. And then affirm it.**

When co-creating a Divine Plan, don't underestimate the universe's ability to bless.

Visualize whatever you desire by seeing the universe's good.

_____
_____
_____
_____
_____
_____
_____
_____
_____
_____
_____
_____

Discuss Giving Way to Growth and Expansion

The process of growth is just as important – and many times much more important – than the end result. Our good cannot be crowded in one instant; we have to be ready for it.

During the time that we wait for our seed-idea of expanded good to take root, to grow in the invisible, to break through skepticism and the past and whatever walls we have built up, we grow. Part of the growth is in allowing the roots, the foundation to build in our subconscious mind. It is a challenge because this is when so many of us give up. But when we learn to enjoy our growth through the process, build our skills, increase our wisdom, uplift our consciousness, we receive our true blessing.

How do you need to grow?

_____
_____
_____
_____
_____
_____
_____
_____
_____
_____
_____
_____
_____
_____

Discuss How You Can Shine Your Light in Gratitude

When problems arise, we cannot judge by appearances but know that there is a blessing in store. Spirit wants us to realign with Divine Source, to realize that when we are challenged, when we are struggling, we have to let go and let God.

Gratitude is not just words of praise, IT IS ENERGY; it activates the spiritual ethers; IT IGNITES THE DIVINE IMPETUS TO FORM AND GIVE SHAPE TO OUR DESIRES.

Thanks makes us open up and ALLOW OUR GOOD because we begin to believe and trust AND KNOW that our good is taking shape. Sometimes we have to be at our lowest to believe we have to rely on a force that is greater than what we see in the physical world.

How can you express your thanks?

_____
_____
_____
_____
_____
_____
_____
_____
_____

Discuss How You Can Give and Receive

If we give – not as a quid pro quo – not expecting something back, we will be blessed. It might not come from the same channel, but it will come back. Giving is a state of consciousness. We are all a part of the continuous flow of God's Good and if we withhold our gifts, if we withhold that which belongs to the universe – out of fear of lack, our life will be thrown off balance, we won't manifest results quickly, and we will experience the appearance of lack in some form.

How can you give?

_____
_____
_____
_____
_____
_____
_____
_____
_____
_____
_____
_____
_____

Discuss How You Can Let Go and Trust the Universe

We may not see behind the scenes, but the universe is building, growing, pruning, shaping, improving, creating, performing, and completing what we are called to do. So, after we have done all – every single thing that we can do, we can let go, and trust that the universe is taking care of the rest.

When a farmer **selects the seed**, that's like us **deciding what we want**. Sometimes, we don't even know what we want. So the first thing that we have to do is be honest about what we want.

When a farmer **prepares the ground for planting,** that's like us praying and **acknowledging the one Source** from which all of our good comes. We never create anything ourselves; the universe is always creating through us. When we acknowledge the Source from which all good comes, then we are filled with the realization that it is inexhaustible.

Planting the seed is when we accept our desires. We plant in the soil of the mind; we plant in the soil of the heart; we plant in the soil of our soul – the **divine idea that is to be made manifest.** The universe is always blessing us with divine ideas, but we have to accept them in order to _plant_ them in our consciousness.

Tending the weeds is when we pour our faith on our goals; when we prune and shape and water the soil through denials and affirmation; when we join together with like-minded people to center; when we journal about it; when we meditate on it.

But after the farmer has selected the seed, prepared the ground, planted the seed and tended the garden, he has to wait. He can't send roots down into the soil. He can't create upward shoots of green. He can't put leafs on the stalks. He can't put blossoms on the flower. _He has to let go and know that natural law is working in cooperation with the seed that is planted to reveal the good that is constantly creating itself in the universal ethers._

What are the various ways in which we can shine our lights by trusting in the universe?

_____
_____
_____
_____
_____
_____
_____
_____
_____
_____
_____
_____
_____
_____
_____

Affirmation of Light

I am centered in the light in me. In the light, I am lifted.

In the light, I am whole.

I of my own self am nothing; the light of the universe shines as me.

I am the light of the world.
My light cannot be hidden.
I give light to all in the house.

I let my light shine before all so that they may see my good works.

No matter what, I keep shining my light.

9 THE LAW OF ACCEPTING OUR VICTORY

"God always knows what you are in need of before you even ask," Dale had said. "Moreover, your highest self, that absolute good within you is always directing you and guiding you. All you have to do is listen. Just shut up and listen." So in the middle of Najih's prayers, he would stop and just listen. . . . Then one day, in the silence, he internalized the all-encompassing power of Spirit everywhere present. He felt secure in that instant – at peace, connected with the unlimited love of strength and power and success. He felt victory filling his body – with a tingling sensation of expectancy. He began to expect the best. His feeling of expectancy wasn't related to something in the flesh or the physical – the material – as Dale called it. It was a connection with the unlimited resource of the universe, a connection with inexhaustible supply that he had never felt before. He began to realize that power was not just within him, it was everywhere present.

Victory is neither here nor there, it is within us. There is no place where we are that it is not. Victory is in the air that we breathe and the space that we take up – making our lives so exceptional that others marvel at where we are. We walk through doors of opportunity that before seemed impossible to open. We cross the ultimate threshold of our faith.

Now is the time. Today is the day. This is the moment in which we do what we have been waiting to do. This is the moment that our goals meet us at the manifestation of our desires.

We must leave our feelings of inadequacy, lack, doubt, fear – and claim our victory. We cast the most important vote of our life – not for a president, proposition or bailout, but for the good that we can do. The fact that everything is unraveling before our eyes points to one conclusion: this is our moment. This is our time to get up and unglue ourselves from whatever was holding us back.

This is our time – not just to watch the world turn but to walk through the open door of creativity, power and strength; to become part of the solution rather than part of the problem. This is our time – not just to stand by watching "hope and change" but to become part of its mandate – by giving and receiving in a new consciousness, the true spirit of my higher consciousness, which has no limitation in the material world.

This is our time – not just to spew the rhetoric of peace but to really do what Thich Nhat Hanh, a famous Buddhist monk, said – to "be peace in every step that we take." This is our time – not just to see the dreams of others reclaimed but to do as Paramahansa Yogananda, a renowned Hindu leader, taught – the work that each one of us were called to do through many lives leading to this one.

Complete the Victory Affirmation

Victory is neither here nor there, it is within me. There is no place where I am that it is not. Victory is in the air that I breathe and the space that I take up – making my life so exceptional that others marvel at where I am.

_____

_____

_____

_____

_____

I walk through doors of opportunity that before seemed impossible to open. I cross the ultimate threshold of my faith.

Now is the time. Today is the day. This is the moment in which I do what I have been waiting to do.

_____

_____

_____

_____

_____

Goals that I believed I had to meet, meet me at the threshold of this new day.

_____

_____

_____

_____

I leave my feelings of inadequacy, my feelings of lack, my feelings of doubt, my feelings of fear – and claim my victory.

_____

_____

_____

_____

_____

I no longer mock Divine Source by asking what the future has in store for me, but I affirm as a true visionary what I have in store for the future. I light my torch of liberty, by realizing that there is nothing that I cannot do.

_____

_____

_____

_____

_____

I become a believer once again. I live without worry and suffering.

I sound the glorious sound of the trumpet, blowing through the land without stopping – until I know the truth and find power pushing me toward my goals.

Today, I claim my victory.

10 THE LAW OF DOING EVEN GREATER THINGS

"I'm so glad I saw you because I almost texted you last night to tell you the good news," Nala said. "I also wanted to tell you," and she paused, as though she was about to say something that was difficult for her to say, "I realized something else about what we were talking about the other night — something else about doing 'even greater things.' "

"What?" asked Najih. He was curious to know because the tenth law of unlimited success was the "Law of Doing Even Greater Things."

"Well, this is what Spirit gave me," Nala always talked about what "Spirit" revealed to her. "The greater things that we must do is not merely to understand spiritual law but to realize that we are the law. The principles of life, the laws of success — are embodied in us."

We all think that only the prophets and the saints of yesterday have the ability to do great things. But at least one of them said that we will do even greater things. This law mandates that we have the capacity to accomplish more than has ever been realized, more than has ever been imagined. Doing greater things demands that we take life by its endless channels and mold it and shape it and co-create it into what we want. Technology has already shown us that we are increasingly enlarging our universe through change and transformation. Doing greater things demands that we step out of the temporary holding patterns of life and start being better than we have ever anticipated. The universe is always creating as us and expressing through us.

Not only each day, but each moment blesses us with a gift to start anew — to do something greater than anything that has ever been done. It doesn't matter what we call God — be it Allah, Buddha, Jehovah, Yahweh, Krishna, or Ra — what matters is whether we have looked in the mirror to love the God in us — to nurture the presence and the power and the peace and the greater things in us. How phenomenal it is to look into the mirror of our lives and see that we are the substance of life — and that just by loving ourselves, we can see absolute good in all things — and *know* that WE are its co-creative force.

We must harness energy in a time and a place that we cannot even imagine, where people fly in the air and speak from devices on their ear and pass the images of movement and music and ministry through computerized images and understand that they are the energy of a vortex that is without limitation. We are at the point of departure, the point of manifestation, the point of demonstrating all that the universe is. We wear the blessing, breathe the blessing, synthesize, materialize and demonstrate the blessing.

EVEN GREATER THINGS EXERCISE

Give each person in your group the three goals that you have been working on; the other person or group has to come up with the greater things that you shall do.

The other person or group has to create the affirmation that you must recite.

The other person or the group must envision you doing the even greater things.

Finally, the person who created the goals must take what others have been working on and adopt them as their own.

EVEN GREATER THINGS LETTER

Write a letter to yourself, envisioning the future and the greater things that you will be able to accomplish. Set forth what you will do based on your dreams, deeply-held desires, prayers, wishes, and previous affirmations.

Dear_____:

_____

_____

_____

EVEN GREATER THINGS MEDITATION

MEDITATE ON MEETING YOUR OLDER SELF – 30-40 YEARS FROM NOW.
ASK THE QUESTIONS THAT YOU HAVE; RESOLVE YOUR ANXIETY ABOUT SUCCESS.

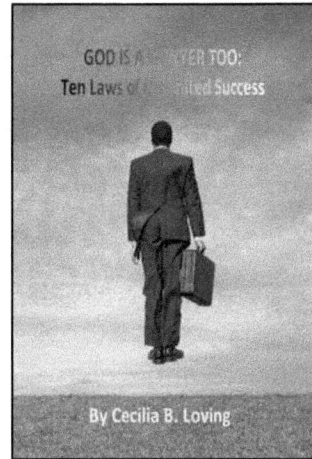

ABOUT THE AUTHOR

Reverend Cecilia Loving is Pastor of SPIRITMUV®, a non-denominational church in New York City (www.spiritmuv.com). She is also the author of *Prayers for Those Standing on the Edge of Greatness, God is a Brown Girl Too,* the *God is a Brown Girl Too Workbooks,* and *God is a Lawyer Too: Ten Laws of Unlimited Success,* as well as the editor of her mother Myrtle Ross' children's books, *Angels, Angels, Everywhere* and *The Angel Blanket* (www.myrtletreepress.webs.com). Her next book, *God is a Baby Too,* is expected to be published by 2013. Her books may also be purchased at www.godisabrowngirltoo.webs.com, as well as www.prayersontheedge.com, www.amazon.com, and any place where other books are sold.

Rev. Loving has a Juris Doctor degree from New York University School of Law, an M.Div. from New York Theological Seminary, an M.F.A. from UCLA, and a B.F.A. from Howard University. She is a member of the New York and Washington, D.C. bars and serves as an arbitrator, mediator and administrative law judge for several alternative dispute resolution tribunals and a New York City hearing tribunal.

While obtaining her Master of Divinity in 2007, Rev. Loving created *Brown Girl-ology* and held the first God is a Brown Girl Too® Retreat in 2009 (www.godisabrowngirltoo.webs.com). Since then, she holds an annual retreat, teaching women of color to uplift the divine within.

Rev. Loving was born in Detroit, Michigan and now resides in Brooklyn, New York with her husband Marlon Cromwell. She is grateful for Marlon's continuous ministry and support, as well as for the support of her parents Myrtle and Hicey Ross, and her other family and friends who helped with the book in so many ways. She is especially thankful for the support of Vaughn Browne, who worked tirelessly to help proof it, as well as for the help of Haneefah Jackson, Femi Austin, Denise Quarles, Elizabeth Walker, Lorraine Dowd-Snella, and Carla Loving, whose watchful eyes and loving support helped usher it into creation. Last but not least, Rev. Loving thanks Rick Taylor, her copy editor – who always blesses her words.

www.ingramcontent.com/pod-product-compliance
Lightning Source LLC
Chambersburg PA
CBHW081526040426
42447CB00013B/3358